Pennsylvania Family Law is Fucking Bullshit

By Mark Harry Forster

Contents

1. **Sample Petition to Reduce Support**

IN THE COURT OF COMMON PLEAS OF ███████ COUNTY, PENNSYLVANIA
SUPPORT DIVISION

███████████████	:	**Docket No.** ████████████
Plaintiff/Respondent	:	
	:	
v.	:	**PACSES Case No.** ██████████
	:	
███████████████	:	
Defendant/Petitioner	:	**IN SUPPORT**

PETITION TO MODIFY SUPPPORT

NOW COMES the Petitioner, ███████████████████████, who respectfully represents:

1. Plaintiff, ██████████████████ (hereinafter referred to as "Respondent"), date of birth ██████████, SSN ██████████, resides at ████████████████████████, and is represented by ████████████████████, Esquire.
2. Defendant, ████████████████ (hereinafter referred to as "Petitioner"), is acting *pro se*.
3. On ████████████, the parties entered into an Agreed Order of Support for the minor child of the parties, ██████████████████████, date of birth ██████████, which directed *inter alia* that Petitioner pay ████ per month for child support and ███ per month to liquidate arrears when applicable. A true and correct copy of the Agreed Order is attached hereto and incorporated herein by reference as Exhibit "A."
4. Since entry of the said Order, the following material and substantial changes in circumstance have occurred:
   a. Respondent's income has increased and the tier of fact will show that her earning capacity is above her actual income due to her education and training.
   b. Petitioner has increased child care expenses which are necessary to maintain employment and appropriate education in pursuit of income while Respondent's actual child care expenses have reduced.
   c. The child's best interests are served by changing the Support Order insomuch as the parties share custody.
   d. Respondent is the sole recipient of the Federal Child Dependency Tax Credit Exemption but a fair division of the same would maximize the total income available to the parties and child.
   e. Petitioner requests a variation from Guidelines pursuant to Rule 1910.16-5 due to his unusual needs and unusual fixed obligations, lack of assets, and overly burdensome liabilities compared to the Respondent's sizeable assets, limited liabilities, and additional income in the Respondent's household.

WHEREFORE, Petitioner respectfully requests a trial before this Honorable Court due to the above to modify the present Support Order.

Respectfully Submitted,

████████████

_____
Date

VERIFICATION

I, ████████████████████, verify that the statements made in this document are true and correct. I understand that false statements herein are made subject to the penalties of 18 Pennsylvania C. S. Section 4904 relating to unsworn falsification to authorities.

_____	████████████████████
Date	

2. Sample of Appeal of a Custody Order

IN THE COURT OF COMMON PLEAS OF ▮▮▮▮ **COUNTY, PENNSYLVANIA**
FAMILY DIVISION

▮▮▮▮▮▮▮▮	:	
Plaintiff/Appellant	:	No. ▮▮▮▮▮▮
	:	
vs.	:	
	:	
▮▮▮▮▮▮▮	:	
Defendant/Appellee	:	
	:	**IN CUSTODY.**

NOTICE OF APPEAL

Notice is hereby given that ▮▮▮▮▮▮▮▮▮▮▮▮, Plaintiff above named, hereby

appeals to the Supreme Court of Pennsylvania from the order entered in this matter on the

_____ day of _____ 20____. This order has been entered in the docket as

evidenced by the attached copy of the docket entry. Pursuant to Pa.R.A.P. 904(c), I, ▮▮▮▮▮▮

▮▮▮▮▮▮, certify that the Request for Transcript is attached. Further, pursuant to Pa.R.A.P.

904(f), I certify that this matter is a Children's Fast Track Appeal.

Respectfully submitted,

By: _____

▮▮▮▮▮▮▮▮▮

Dated: _____   Ph: ▮▮▮▮▮▮▮

IN THE COURT OF COMMON PLEAS OF ███████ **COUNTY, PENNSYLVANIA**
FAMILY DIVISION

████████████████	:	
Plaintiff/Appellant	:	**No.** ████████
	:	
vs.	:	
	:	
████████████	:	
Defendant/Appellee	:	
	:	**IN CUSTODY.**

ORDER FOR TRANSCRIPT

A Notice of Appeal – Children's Fast Track having been filed in this matter, the official

court reporter is hereby Ordered to produce, certify and file the transcript in this matter in

conformity with Rule 1922 of the Pennsylvania Rules of Appellate Procedure.

_____
J.

IN THE COURT OF COMMON PLEAS OF ███████ COUNTY, PENNSYLVANIA
FAMILY DIVISION

████████████████	:	
Plaintiff/Appellant	:	**No.** ██████████
	:	
vs.	:	
	:	
████████████	:	
Defendant/Appellee	:	
_____ :		**IN CUSTODY.**

PROOF OF SERVICE

I, ████████████████, do hereby certify that on the _____ day of

_____, 20___, I served true and correct copies of the Notice of Appeal –

Children's Fast Track, Request for Transcript, and Notice of Matters Complained of on Appeal

to the following parties, which service satisfied the requirements of Pa.R.A.P. 121:

<u>Via USPS Certified Mail # & Email</u>

████████████████

Email: ████████████

<u>Via USPS Certified Mail #, Fax & Email</u>

███████████████, Esq.

Law Office of ████████

██████████████

Fax: ████████

Email: ████████████

<u>Via USPS Certified Mail #, Fax & Email</u>

The Honorable ████████████

Court of Common Pleas of ██████ County, Domestic Relations Section

████████████

Fax: ████████

Email: ███████████████████████

<u>Via USPS Certified Mail #</u>
_, Court Reporter
Court of Common Pleas of ████ County

Dated: _____

IN THE SUPREME COURT OF PENNSYLVANIA

▮▮▮▮▮▮▮▮▮	:	
Plaintiff/Appellant	:	**No.**
	:	
vs.	:	
	:	
▮▮▮▮▮▮▮	:	
Defendant/Appellee	:	

JURISDICTIONAL STATEMENT REQUIRED BY RULE 909

Pursuant to Pennsylvania Rules of Appellate Procedure 909 and 910, Appellant ▮▮▮▮ ▮▮▮▮ (hereinafter referred to as "Appellant"), submits this Jurisdictional Statement in support of his Notice of Appeal from the Court of Common Pleas in ▮▮▮▮▮▮▮.

I.   OPINION BELOW

This is an appeal from the order entered by the Court of Common Pleas of ▮▮▮ County, Pennsylvania in ▮▮▮▮▮ entered by Judge ▮▮▮▮▮▮▮ on _____. A copy of the _____ order is attached hereto as Exhibit A.

II.   BASIS FOR JURISDICTION OF THE SUPREME COURT

The Supreme Court of Pennsylvania has jurisdiction over the present appeal pursuant to Pennsylvania Rules of Appellate Procedure 904, 905, 1112, 1925, 1931, and 2172.

III.   TEXT OF ORDERS IN QUESTION

Petitioner seeks review of the entire Order of the Court of Common Pleas of ▮▮▮ County, Pennsylvania, Family Division. A copy of the _____ order is attached hereto as Exhibit A.

IV.   CONCISE STATEMENT OF PROCEDURAL HISTORY

On ████████████, Appellant filed a Petition for Modification of a Custody Order.
An Order was entered fixing a Custody Conference for ████████████. The
Report of the Custody Conference Officer was entered on the same date. On
████████████, an Order was entered approving Stipulation of Counsel for ████
████ to conduct a custody evaluation.

V.   QUESTIONS PRESENTED FOR REVIEW

1. Did the Court of Common Pleas err as a matter of law when it failed to consider the
   factors delineated in the child custody statute prior to awarding primary
   physical custody of child to Appellee?

   SUGGESTED ANSWER: Yes.

2. Did the Court of Common Pleas err as a matter of law when it held that evidence was
   sufficient to support a determination that the child custody factor that … favored
   Appellee?

   SUGGESTED ANSWER: Yes.

3. Was the Court of Common Pleas' award of primary custody of child to Appellee
   unreasonable in light of its factual findings?

   SUGGESTED ANSWER: Yes.

4. Do the remarks of the trial court judge regarding Appellant establish an appearance of
   impropriety such that the decisions regarding custody were the result of bias?

   SUGGESTED ANSWER: Yes.

5. Did the Court of Common Pleas err by depriving Appellant of liberty and fundamental
   rights under color of law by depriving him of the fundamental right to the care, custody

and control of his minor child without affording him the procedural protections guaranteed by the United States Constitution?

SUGGESTER ANSWER: Yes.

6. Did the Court of Common Pleas err by establishing policies, procedures, and precedents denying parents a full and prompt hearing when stripping one parent of adequate physical custody in violation of the Fourteenth Amendment to the United States' Constitution?

SUGGESTED ANSWER: Yes.

WHEREFORE, Appellant requests that this Court reverse and remand the Court of Common Pleas' _____ decision in this matter.

Respectfully submitted,

By: _____

Ph:
Fax:

IN THE COURT OF COMMON PLEAS OF ▮▮▮▮ **COUNTY, PENNSYLVANIA**
FAMILY DIVISION

▮▮▮▮▮▮▮▮▮	:	
Plaintiff/Appellant	:	**No.** ▮▮▮▮▮▮
	:	
vs.	:	
	:	
▮▮▮▮▮▮▮	:	
Defendant/Appellee	:	
	:	**IN CUSTODY.**

PLAINTIFF/APPELLANT'S CONCISE
STATEMENT OF ERRORS COMPLAINED OF ON APPEAL

AND NOW Comes the Plaintiff/Appellant, ▮▮▮▮▮▮▮▮▮▮, and respectfully files this

Concise Statement of Errors Complained of on Appeal pursuant to the Pennsylvania Rules of

Appellate Procedure.

The Defendant responds timely to the Order of _____

issued and signed by the Honorable ▮▮▮▮▮▮▮▮ to file of record a Concise Statement of

Errors Complained of On Appeal pursuant to Pennsylvania Rule of Appellate Procedure 1925(b).

Plaintiff/Appellant filed a Notice of Appeal on _____ which

was accepted and docketed by the Court of Common Pleas of ▮▮▮▮ County, Pennsylvania. This

Appeal is a Children's Fast Track Appeal.

ARGUEMENT

A. THE TRIAL COURT ERRED AND ABUSED ITS DISCRETION BY FAILING TO
   CONSIDER THE FACTORS DELINEATED IN THE CHILD CUSTODY STATUE
   PRIOR TO AWARDING PRIMARY PHYSICAL CUSTODY TO APPELLEE.

When reviewing a child custody order the Superior Court may reject the conclusions of the

trial court only if they involve an error of law, or are unreasonable in light of the sustainable

findings of the trial court. The Superior Court is not bound by the trial court's deductions or inferences from its factual findings. *J.R.M. v. J.E.A.*, 33 A.3d 647 (Pa., 2011). The Superior

Court may reject the conclusions of the trial court if they involve an error of law, or are

unreasonable in light of the sustainable findings of the trial court. The best-interests standard,

applied in a child custody modification proceeding and decided on a case-by-case

basis, considers all factors that legitimately have an effect upon the child's physical, intellectual,

moral, and spiritual well-being. *R.S. v. T.T.*, 113 A.3d 1254 (Pa., 2015).

B. THE TRIAL COURT ERRED AS A MATTER OF LAW WHEN IT HELD THAT
   EVIDENCE WAS SUFFICIENT TO SUPPORT A DETERMINATION THAT
   THE CHILD CUSTODY FACTOR THAT … FAVORED APPELLEE

C. THE COURT OF COMMON PLEAS' AWARD OF PRIMARY CUSTODY OF CHILD
   TO APPELLEE WAS UNREASONABLE IN LIGHT OF ITS FACTUAL FINDINGS

D. THE REMARKS OF THE TRIAL COURT JUDGE REGARDING APPELLANT
   ESTABLISH AN APPEARANCE OF IMPROPRIETY SUCH THAT THE DECISIONS
   REGARDING CUSTODY WERE THE RESULT OF BIAS

E. THE COURT OF COMMON PLEAS ERRED BY DEPRIVING APPELLANT OF
   LIBERTY AND FUNDAMENTAL RIGHTS UNDER COLOR OF LAW BY
   DEPRIVING HIM OF THE FUNDAMENTAL RIGHT TO THE CARE, CUSTODY
   AND CONTROL OF HIS MINOR CHILD WITHOUT AFFORDING HIM THE
   PROCEDURAL PROTECTIONS GUARANTEED BY THE UNITED STATES
   CONSTITUTION

F. THE COURT OF COMMON PLEAS ERRED BY ESTABLISHING POLICIES,
   PROCEDURES, AND PRECEDENTS DENYING PARENTS A FULL AND PROMPT
   HEARING WHEN STRIPPING ONE PARENT OF ADEQUATE PHYSICAL
   CUSTODY IN VIOLATION OF THE FOURTEENTH AMENDMENT TO THE
   UNITED STATES' CONSTITUTION

Respectfully submitted,

By: _____

Ph:
Fax:

IN THE COURT OF COMMON PLEAS OF ███ **COUNTY, PENNSYLVANIA**
FAMILY DIVISION

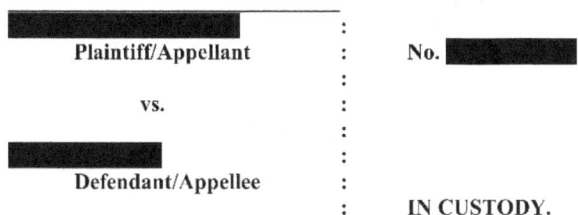

███	:	**No.** ███
Plaintiff/Appellant	:	
	:	
vs.	:	
	:	
███	:	
Defendant/Appellee	:	
	:	**IN CUSTODY.**

CERTIFICATE OF SERVICE

I, ███, hereby certify that I served the foregoing _ on the following parties

via first class mail and USPS Certified Mail:

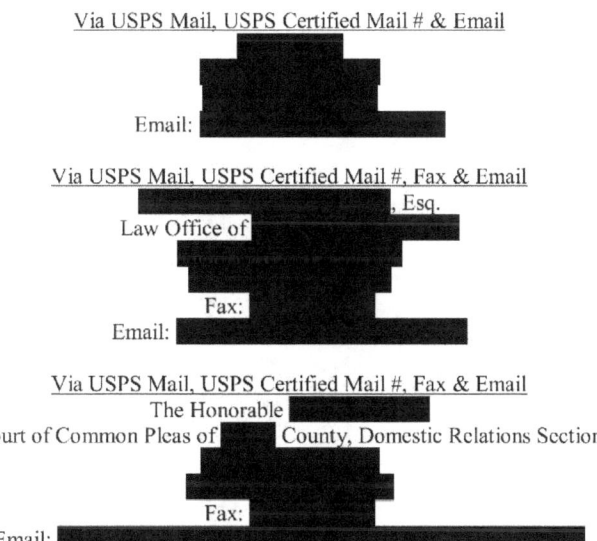

Via USPS Mail, USPS Certified Mail # & Email

Email: ███

Via USPS Mail, USPS Certified Mail #, Fax & Email

███, Esq.

Law Office of ███

Fax: ███

Email: ███

Via USPS Mail, USPS Certified Mail #, Fax & Email

The Honorable ███

Court of Common Pleas of ███ County, Domestic Relations Section

Fax: ███

Email: ███

Via USPS Mail & USPS Certified Mail #
_, Court Reporter
Court of Common Pleas of ███ County

Dated: _____   _____

3. Funny Support Check and Response

Apply to account:

DATE

PAY
TO
THE
ORDER
OF
THE BLOOD SUCKING SCUM AT PENNSYLVANIA SCDU

AMOUNT

**$

Void After 90 Days   MP

PENNSYLVANIA
STATE COLLECTION AND DISBURSEMENT UNIT

NOTICE of Returned Support Check

The Pennsylvania State Collection and Disbursement Unit (PA SCDU) is unable to process the enclosed payment, check # ███████████████. It could not be processed due to the following discrepancy: **Not Payable to PA SCDU**

Please note that altered checks, including alterations that have been initialed, will be returned to you for reissue of a new check. **To ensure processing of your payment, the defendant's full name, SSN and/or the PACSES ten digit Member ID number must be included.**

If you have questions regarding these or any matters pertaining to PA SCDU, please call Customer Service at the number provided below. You may be required by Pennsylvania state law to remit support electronically. Contact the Customer Service number below for more information.

Defendant Customer Service (877)727-7238
Please return Defendant payments to:
PASCDU
P.O. Box 69110
Harrisburg, PA 17106-9110

Employer Customer Service (877)676-9580
Please return Employer payments to:
PASCDU
P.O. Box 69112
Harrisburg, PA 17106-9112

Sincerely,
Pennsylvania State Collection and Disbursement Unit

4. <u>Sample Income Withholding Order</u>

What gets mailed to your employer, so that they garnish your wages for child support.

INCOME WITHHOLDING FOR SUPPORT

○ ORIGINAL INCOME WITHHOLDING ORDER/NOTICE FOR SUPPORT (IWO)
◉ AMENDED IWO
○ ONE-TIME ORDER/NOTICE FOR LUMP SUM PAYMENT
○ TERMINATION OF IWO

Date: ___01/26/18___

| ☐ Child Support Enforcement (CSE) Agency | ☒ Court | ☐ Attorney | ☐ Private Individual/Entity (Check One) |

NOTE: This IWO must be regular on its face. Under certain circumstances you must reject this IWO and return it to the sender (see IWO instructions **http://www.acf.hhs.gov/programs/css/resource/income-withholding-for-support-instructions**). If you receive this document from someone other than a state or tribal CSE agency or a court, a copy of the underlying order must be attached.

State/Tribe/Territory Commonwealth of Pennsylvania
City/County/Dist./Tribe ▓▓▓▓▓
Private Individual/Entity _____

Remittance ID (include w/payment): ▓▓▓▓▓
Order ID: *(See Addendum for order/docket information)*
CSE Agency Case ID: *(See Addendum for case summary)*

RE: ▓▓▓▓▓

Employee/Obligor's Name (Last, First, Middle)
▓▓▓▓▓

Employee/Obligor's Social Security Number

(See Addendum for plaintiff names
associated with cases on attachment)

Custodial Party/Obligee's Name (Last, First, Middle)

Employer/Income Withholder's FEIN _____

Child(ren)'s Name(s) (Last, First, Middle)   Child(ren)'s Birth Date(s)

_____   _____
_____   _____
_____   _____
_____   _____
_____   _____

NOTE: This IWO must be regular on its face. Under certain circumstances you must reject this IWO and return it to the sender (see IWO instructions http://www.acf.hhs.gov/programs/css/resource/income-withholding-for-support-instructions). If you receive this document from someone other than a state or tribal CSE agency or a court, a copy of the underlying order must be attached.

7122100332

See Addendum for dependent names and birth dates associated with cases on attachment.

ORDER INFORMATION: This document is based on the support or withholding order from ▓▓▓▓▓ County, Commonwealth of Pennsylvania (State/Tribe). You are required by law to deduct these amounts from the employee/obligor's income until further notice.

$ ___▓▓▓▓___ per month in current child support
$ ___0.00___ per month in past-due child support - **Arrears greater than 12 weeks?** ○ yes ◉ no
$ ___0.00___ per month in current cash medical support
$ ___0.00___ per month in past-due cash medical support
$ ___0.00___ per month in current spousal support
$ ___0.00___ per month in past-due spousal support
$ ___0.00___ per month in other (must specify) _____.

for a **Total Amount to Withhold of** $ ___▓▓▓▓___ per month.

AMOUNTS TO WITHHOLD: You do not have to vary your pay cycle to be in compliance with the *Order Information*. If your pay cycle does not match the ordered payment cycle, withhold one of the following amount:

$ ___▓▓▓___ per weekly pay period. $ ___▓▓▓___ per semimonthly pay period (twice a month)
$ ___▓▓▓___ per biweekly pay period (every two weeks) $ ___▓▓▓___ per monthly pay period.
$ _____ **Lump Sum Payment:** Do not stop any existing IWO unless you receive a termination order.

REMITTANCE INFORMATION: If the employee/obligor's principal place of employment is within the Commonwealth of Pennsylvania (State/Tribe), you must begin withholding no later than the first pay period that occurs ten (10) working days after the date of this Order/Notice. Send payment within seven (7) working days of the pay date. If you cannot withhold the full amount of support for any or all orders for this employee/obligor, withhold up to 55% of disposable income for all orders. If the employee/obligor's principal place of employment is not within the Commonwealth of Pennsylvania (State/Tribe), obtain withholding limitations, time requirements, and any allowable employer fees at www.acf.hhs.gov/programs/css/resource/state-income-withholding-contacts-and-program-information for the employee/obligor's principal place of employment.

Document Tracking Identifier _____

OMB No.: 0970-0154

Form EN-028 04/16
Worker ID $IATT

Service Type M

Employer's Name: ████████████████

Employer FEIN: _____

Employee/Obligor's Name: ████████████████   SSN: ████████

CSE Agency Case Identifier: *(See Addendum for case summary)*   Order Identifier: *(See Addendum for order/docket information)*

☐ **Return to Sender [Completed by Employer/Income Withholder].** Payment must be directed to an SDU in accordance with 42 USC §666(b)(5) and (b)(6) or tribal Payee (see Payments to SDU below). If payment is not directed to an SDU/tribal Payee or this IWO is not regular on its face, you *must* check this box and return the IWO to the sender.

Signature of Judge/Issuing Official (if required by State or Tribal law): _____ *JAMES M MCMASTER*
Print Name of Judge/Issuing Official: _____
Title of Judge/Issuing Official: _____
Date of Signature: _____ JANUARY 26, 2018

If the employee/obligor works in a state or for a tribe that is different from the state or tribe that issued this order, a copy of this IWO must be provided to the employee/obligor.

☐ If checked, the employer/income withholder must provide a copy of this form to the employee/obligor.

ADDITIONAL INFORMATION FOR EMPLOYERS/INCOME WITHHOLDERS

Pennsylvania law (23 PA C.S. § 4374(b)) requires remittance by an <u>electronic payment method</u> if an employer is ordered to withhold income from more than one employee and employs 15 or more persons, or if an employer has a history of two or more returned checks due to nonsufficient funds. Please call the Pennsylvania State Collections and Disbursement Unit (PA SCDU) Employer Customer Service at 1-877-676-9580 for instructions. PA FIPS CODE 42 000 00

Make Remittance Payable to: PA SCDU

Send check to: Pennsylvania SCDU, P.O. Box 69112, Harrisburg, Pa 17106-9112

IN ADDITION, PAYMENTS MUST INCLUDE THE DEFENDANT'S NAME AND THE PACSES MEMBER ID (shown above as the Employee/Obligor's Case Identifier) OR SOCIAL SECURITY NUMBER IN ORDER TO BE PROCESSED. DO NOT SEND CASH BY MAIL.

State-specific contact and withholding information can be found on the Federal Employer Services website located at:
www.acf.hhs.gov/programs/css/resource/state-income-withholding-contacts-and-program-information

Priority: Withholding for support has priority over any other legal process under state law against the same income (42 USC §666(b)(7)). If a federal tax levy is in effect, please notify the sender.

Combining Payments: When remitting payments to an SDU or tribal CSE agency, you may combine withheld amounts from more than one employee/obligor's income in a single payment. You must, however, separately identify each employee/obligor's portion of the payment.

Payments To SDU: You must send child support payments payable by income withholding to the appropriate SDU or to a tribal CSE agency. If this IWO instructs you to send a payment to an entity other than an SDU (e.g., payable to the custodial party, court, or attorney), you must check the box above and return this notice to the sender. Exception: If this IWO was sent by a court, attorney, or private individual/entity and the initial order was entered before January 1, 1994 or the order was issued by a tribal CSE agency, you must follow the "Remit payment to" instructions on this form.

Reporting the Pay Date: You must report the pay date when sending the payment. The pay date is the date on which the amount was withheld from the employee/obligor's wages. You must comply with the law of the state (or tribal law if applicable) of the employee/obligor's principal place of employment regarding time periods within which you must implement the withholding and forward the support payments.

Multiple IWOs: If there is more than one IWO against this employee/obligor and you are unable to fully honor all IWOs due to federal, state, or tribal withholding limits, you must honor all IWOs to the greatest extent possible, giving priority to current support before payment of any past-due support. Follow the state or tribal law/procedure of the employee/obligor's principal place of employment to determine the appropriate allocation method.

Lump Sum Payments: You may be required to notify a state or tribal CSE agency of upcoming lump sum payments to this employee/obligor such as bonuses, commissions, or severance pay. Contact the sender to determine if you are required to report and/or withhold lump sum payments.

Liability: If you have any doubts about the validity of this IWO, contact the sender. If you fail to withhold income from the employee/obligor's income as the IWO directs, you are liable for both the accumulated amount you should have withheld and any penalties set by state or tribal law/procedure. _____

OMB Expiration Date – 07/31/2017. The OMB Expiration Date has no bearing on the termination date of the IWO. It identifies the version of the form currently in use.

Service Type M   Page 2 of 3

Form EN-028 04/16
Worker ID $IATT

Employer's Name: ███████████████████████   Employer FEIN: _____

Employee/Obligor's Name: ███████████████   ███████ SSN: ██████████

CSE Agency Case Identifier: *(See Addendum for case summary)*   Order Identifier: *(See Addendum for order/docket information)*

Anti-discrimination: You are subject to a fine determined under state or tribal law for discharging an employee/obligor from employment, refusing to employ, or taking disciplinary action against an employee/obligor because of this IWO.

_____

Withholding Limits: You may not withhold more than the lesser of: 1) the amounts allowed by the Federal Consumer Credit Protection Act (CCPA) (15 USC §1673(b)); or 2) the amounts allowed by the state of the employee/obligor's principal place of employment or tribal law if a tribal order (see *Remittance Information*). Disposable income is the net income after mandatory deductions such as: state, federal, local taxes; Social Security taxes; statutory pension contributions; and Medicare taxes. The federal limit is 50% of the disposable income if the obligor is supporting another family and 60% of the disposable income if the obligor is not supporting another family. However, those limits increase 5% - to 55% and 65% - if the arrears are greater than 12 weeks. If permitted by the state or tribe, you may deduct a fee for administrative costs. The combined support amount and fee may not exceed the limit indicated in this section.

For tribal orders, you may not withhold more than the amounts allowed under the law of the issuing tribe. For tribal employers/income withholders who receive a state IWO, you may not withhold more than the limit set by tribal law.

Depending upon applicable state or tribal law, you may need to also consider the amounts paid for health care premiums in determining disposable income and applying appropriate withholding limits.

Arrears greater than 12 weeks? If the *Order Information* does not indicate that the arrears are greater than 12 weeks, then the Employer should calculate the CCPA limit using the lower percentage.

Supplemental Information: _____

_____

_____

NOTIFICATION OF EMPLOYMENT TERMINATION OR INCOME STATUS: If this employee/obligor never worked for you or you are no longer withholding income for this employee/obligor, you must promptly notify the CSE agency and/or the sender by returning this form to the address listed in the Contact Information below: 7122100332

○ This person has never worked for this employer nor received periodic income.

○ This person no longer works for this employer nor receives periodic income.

Please provide the following information for the employee/obligor:

Termination date: _____   Last known phone number: _____

Last known address: _____

_____

Final Payment Date To SDU/tribal payee: _____   Final Payment Amount: _____

New Employer's Name: _____

New Employer's Address: _____

_____

CONTACT INFORMATION:

To Employer/Income Withholder: If you have any questions, contact <u>CLIENT SERVICES UNIT</u> (Issuer name)
by phone: ██████████ , by fax: ██████████ by email or website: www.childsupport.state.pa.us.
Send termination/income status notice and other correspondence to: <u>DOMESTIC RELATIONS SECTION,</u> ███████████
███████████████ (Issuer address).

To Employee/Obligor: If the employee/obligor has questions, contact <u>CLIENT SERVICES UNIT</u> (Issuer name)
by phone: ██████████ , by fax: ██████████ , by email or website: www.childsupport.state.pa.us.

IMPORTANT: The person completing this form is advised that the information may be shared with the employee/obligor.

Service Type M

OMB No.: 0970-0154

Page 3 of 3

Form EN-028 04/16

Worker ID $IATT

ADDENDUM
Summary of Cases on Attachment

Defendant/Obligor: ████████████

PACSES Case Number ████████

Plaintiff Name

████████

Docket ████████   Attachment Amount
$

Child(ren)'s Name(s): ████████████   DOB ████

_____
_____
_____
_____
_____
_____
_____

PACSES Case Number

Plaintiff Name

Docket   Attachment Amount
$ 0.00

Child(ren)'s Name(s):   DOB

_____
_____
_____
_____
_____
_____
_____

PACSES Case Number

Plaintiff Name

Docket   Attachment Amount
$ 0.00

Child(ren)'s Name(s):   DOB

_____
_____
_____
_____
_____
_____
_____

PACSES Case Number

Plaintiff Name

Docket   Attachment Amount
$ 0.00

Child(ren)'s Name(s):   DOB

_____
_____
_____
_____
_____
_____
_____

PACSES Case Number

Plaintiff Name

Docket   Attachment Amount
$ 0.00

Child(ren)'s Name(s):   DOB

_____
_____
_____
_____
_____
_____
_____

PACSES Case Number

Plaintiff Name

Docket   Attachment Amount
$ 0.00

Child(ren)'s Name(s):   DOB

_____
_____
_____
_____
_____
_____
_____

Service Type M

Addendum

OMB No.: 0970-0154

Form EN-028 04/16

Worker ID $IATT

5. A Great Lawsuit Filed in United States District Court for the District of New Jersey

IN THE UNITED STATES DISTRICT COURT
FOR THE DISTRICT OF NEW JERSEY

TUHIN PANDYA for himself and as   )
parent of A.P.,   )
)
      Plaintiffs,   )
)
      v.   )
)
JOSEPH PAONE, in his individual and   )
official capacities   )   Jury trial is requested with respect to all
)   issues so all triable
          Defendant.   )

COMPLAINT

Jurisdiction

1.   This Court has jurisdiction over this matter under 28 U.S.C. §1331. Plaintiffs maintain this action, inter alia, under 42 U.S.C. §1983, and the Declaratory Judgment Act, 28 U.S.C. § 2201. Joseph Paone, in his official and individual capacity deprived Pandya of liberty under color of law by ordering him arrested without due process and without jurisdiction, and further by depriving him of the fundamental right to the care, custody and control of his minor child without affording him even minimal procedural protections guaranteed by the United States Constitution.

Summary

2.   Plaintiffs seek declaratory and injunctive relief as well as monetary damages against Joseph Paone because Judge Paone ordered Pandya arrested without jurisdiction, and without a hearing or even an explanation of why he was ordered to be arrested. Pandya was briefly arrested and taken to the police station but released after a different judge vacated the illegal arrest warrant issued by Judge Paone.

Parties

3.   Tuhin Pandya is an adult residing in Middlesex County. He is father of the minor child A.P.

4.   Defendant Paone is a Superior court judge in Middlesex County. He is sued in his official and individual capacities; by his actions and policies he denied plaintiffs constitutional rights under color of law; he is a person within the meaning of 42 U.S.C. §1983 with respect to declarative and injunctive relief and damages sought in this case.

5.   Judge Paone was first appointed as judge by Governor Jon Corzine in 2010 and assigned to the criminal division. In September 2014 Judge Paone was re-assigned to the family part.

Statement of Facts

6.   Plaintiff Tuhin Pandya was divorced from his wife Roopal Shah in 2013 after he discovered that she had been having an affair with her boss and that she had video recorded some of her sexual encounters with the boss.

7.   Pandya and Shah had one child A.P. . A.P was 12 months old at the time of signing marital settlement agreement.

8.   Pandya and Shah entered into a marital settlement agreement under the terms of which Pandya and Shah had shared legal and physical custody of A.P.

9.   Pandya agreed to allow Shah to exercise the bulk of parenting time with A.P for the next two years during which time Shah would stay at home and care for A.P. and because Shah stated she intended to nurse A.P. for eighteen months.

10.   During this period Pandya's parenting time with A.P. was limited to every other weekend and a few hours one night each week.

11.   In 2014, Shah went to work full-time and put A.P. in daycare.

12.   In September 2014, Shah filed a motion for an increase in child support and also demanding that Pandya pay for day care.

13.   In October 2014 Pandya filed a cross motion demanding equal parenting time, as the initial period during which Pandya had agreed to let Shah exercise most of the parenting time had elapsed and Shah was now relying on daycare.

14.   As of October 2014 A.P. was spending more time in daycare than with his father.

15.   A.P. repeatedly expressed desire to spend more time with his daddy, who he only saw for a few hours a week, especially on "off weeks" when Pandya did not have a weekend visit.

16.   The motion for child support and cross motion for increased parenting time became complicated when Pandya learned that Shah had received a secret payment of at least $400,000 in 2013 from her boss (with whom she had been having an affair). The total amount of the payment is not certain as part was paid in cash.

17.   Shah's case information statement submitted as part of her application to the court for increased child support and increased money for day care stated that Shah had received virtually no money in 2013 and claimed to have a negative net worth, with only $5,000 in the bank

18.   The motion and cross motion was heard by Superior Court Judge Joseph Paone, who had only been assigned to the family division a few weeks earlier.

19.   Judge Paone denied Pandya's application for equal parenting time giving as his reason that Pandya had not established "changed circumstances."   In an order and brief statement of reasons (at least on the equal custody issue), dated October 28, 2014 and distributed November 12, 2014, Judge Paone denied Pandya equal parenting time with A.P. stating that Pandya had failed to meet his burden who that there were "changed circumstances" that affected the welfare of the child.

20.   By implication, Judge Paone ruled that Pandya would be denied equal parenting time indefinitely until Pandya proved changed circumstances affecting the welfare of the child by a preponderance of the evidence.

21.   Again the procedural situation was complicated by Shah's application for increased child support and her concealment of a $400,000 or more payment.

22.   At oral argument on the motion and cross motion counsel for Pandya informed the court that it was known that Shah had obtained a large amount of money from her former employer in 2013. Although Shah's counsel acknowledged there may have been a payment, Pandya was not able at that time to submit any documentation of the amount.

23.   As a result, in the same order in which Judge Paone denied the motion for equal parenting time Judge Paone granted Shah's request for increase in child support.

24.   Pandya was able to obtain a copy of an agreement showing that Shah has obtained at least $400,000 from her former employer in 2013 within a few months of signing the Martial Settlement Agreement.

25.   On December 1, 2014, Pandya filed a motion for reconsideration attaching a copy of the agreement showing a $400,000 payment to Shah by her former employer with whom she had an affair.

26.   From December 2014 forward the child custody and child support issues got separated unto different tracks.

27.   The motion for reconsideration of the child support was granted based on Shah apparently concealing assets, however, Pandya continued to pursue equal time with A.P.

28.   Pandya filed a separate motion with the court demanding equal time with A.P. arguing that he had a fundamental right to the care custody and control of his child, which included equal custody with Shah, and that the state was interfering with this fundamental right.

29.   While the custody motion was still pending Judge Paone ultimately denied Pandya's child support motion ruling, inter alia, that the $400,000 payment would be ignored for child support purposes and that the Settlement Agreement had not been obtained fraudulently by concealing the $400,000 payment.

30.   To preserve this issue, Pandya filed a notice of appeal with the appellate division—again while the parenting time issue was pending.

31.   Judge Paone on May 29, 2015 denied the application for equal parenting time due to lack of jurisdiction. A copy of the Order is attached as Exhibit 1.

32.   Oddly, paragraph 8 of the Order did not deny for lack of jurisdiction, but addressed a part of the cross motion by Shah asking the court to find that Pandya had violated the Settlement Agreement (the legality of which was on appeal).

33.   Paragraph 8 of the Order, however, stated that Shah's motion was "DENIED IN PART as to a finding of a violation." That is, Judge Paone found that Pandya had not violated the agreement (which was on appeal anyway).

34.   Judge Paone's Order clearly acknowledged that he lacked jurisdiction due to the appeal being filed.

35.   No further hearings or proceedings took place in the family court.

36.   According to Justine Abrams, who worked for Paone, Judge Paone went on vacation and was out of the office for all or most of July and August.

37.   On July 30, 2015 Judge Paone signed an arrest warrant that provided:

> You are hereby commanded to arrest (name) Tuhin G. Pandya and confine
> him to the County Jail
> subject has failed to comply with a court order dated 5/29/15 in that
> subject has pending complaints for $250,000 life insurance policy …
> to be detailed until next scheduled court day.

Exhibit 2.

38.   Upon information and belief Judge Paone was on vacation July 31, 2015 and may not have even been within the State of New Jersey or even the United States.

39.   Counsel for Pandya received a copy of the arrest warrant on August 3, 2015 and immediately filed an Order to Show Cause asking that the Warrant be quashed.

40.   The motion on the Order to Show Cause argued inter alia that the Warrant was illegal and unconstitutional as Judge Paone had failed to have a plenary hearing, and had made no findings of fact. Pandya further noted that the New Jersey Supreme Court had also held that a judge could not order a party incarcerated without a finding of a willful refusal to follow a court order. Schochet v. Schochet, 89 A.3d 1264, 1268 (App. Div. 2014).

41.   The arrest warrant was vacated by Judge Christopher Rafano on August 4, 2015, and a copy of the order vacating the arrest warrant was faxed to the Middlesex County Sheriff's Office by Judge Rafano at 5:08 pm on August 4.

42.   Later that evening police officers showed up at Pandya's home to arrest him.

43.   Pandya showed police officers a copy of the court order vacating the arrest warrant, however, police took Pandya into custody while they verified the new order.

44.   Pandya was arrested and placed in handcuffs and taken to the Middlesex County Sheriff's Office.

45.   Pandya was detained at the Middlesex County Sheriff's Office for over an hour but was released and allowed to go home.

Count I

Deprivation of Liberty under Color of Law without Due Process

46.   Pandya re-alleges previous paragraphs as fully restated.

47.   Defendant Judge Paone signed an arrest warrant depriving Pandya of liberty without due process.

48.   There was no finding of fact that Pandya had violated any court order; in fact, the May 29, 2015 Order and Statement of reasons found that there had been no violation by Pandya.

49.   Moreover there was no finding of a willful violation and no plenary hearing.   An "ability to comply" hearing is required prior to a judge issuing an arrest warrant and making finding that there is a willful refusal to comply with a court order. Schochet v. Schochet, 89 A.3d 1264, 1268 (App. Div. 2014).

50.   The requirement that an arrest order not be issued without a hearing at which a willful refusal is prove appears to be a requirement of due process under the Fourteenth Amendment to the United States Constitution.

51.   Although the Third Circuit has held that no hearing is required to issue a bench warrant for failure to appear, the Court has explained that failure to appear for a valid warrant constitutes probably cause for a warrant. In re Grand Jury Proceedings Harrisburg Grand Jury 79-1, 658 F.2d 211, 214 (3d Cir. 1981) ("The simple fact of nonappearance provided the government with probable cause to apply for a bench warrant for McNabb.")

52.   In the instant case there was no finding of probable cause, Judge Paone appears to have signed the arrest warrant without any findings, and did so while on vacation.

53.   More importantly, Judge Paone lacked jurisdiction to issue the Order. Judge Paone's Court had lost jurisdiction over the matter as a result of the appeal.

54.   Judge Paone knew very well he lacked jurisdiction as he himself has stated that he could not grant Pandya additional parenting time because his court lacked jurisdiction over the matter as a result of the appeal.

55.   The arrest warrant purported to be enforcing a May 29, 2015 Order, but the case was on appeal as of May 29, 2015 and thus the Court had no jurisdiction to enforce any such Order.

56.   Because Judge Paone's court lacked jurisdiction Joseph Paone is not entitled to judicial immunity and is subject to damages. Mireles v. Waco, 502 U.S. 9, 12 (1991).

Relief

WHEREFORE, Pandya requests:

Damages as determined by a jury;

Costs and attorneys' fees as provided under federal law;

Declaratory and injunctive relief that bench warrants may not issue without a finding of probable cause of a willful violation;

Such other relief as the Court determines to be just and appropriate.

Count II

Declaratory and Injunctive Relief against Judge Paone and any successors Declaring that parents have a fundamental constitutional right to equal custody of children which may not be denied without a finding of abuse or neglect

57.   Plaintiffs re-allege previous paragraphs as fully restated.

58.   The Appellate Division has now granted a limited remand for the trial court to address parenting time and parenting time only, however, as of this filing no action has been taken.

59.   A.P. is not yet four years old. Pandya has been seeking equal custody for nearly a year now, thus for more than 25% of his life, A.P. has been limited to seeing his daddy on average one day a week because Judge Paone refuses to recognize the fundamental right of Pandya to equal physical custody of A.P.

60.   Judge Paone on October 28, 2015 denied Pandya and A.P equal physical custody claiming that Pandya was required to show changed circumstances.

61.   This ruling was apparently based on a widespread policy in New Jersey family courts that parents in a custody dispute have no fundamental rights. In Sacharow v. Sacharow, 826 A.2d 710, 721 (N.J. 2003) the New Jersey Supreme Court held that

> [W]hen, as here, both parents have a fundamental right to the care and nurturing of their children and neither has a preeminent right over the other, their contest stands on different footing. It is not a third party or the State that seeks to intrude into the protected sphere of family autonomy. Rather, by submitting their dispute to the court, it is the parties themselves who essentially seek the impairment of each other's rights. ... In such cases, the sole benchmark is the best interests of the child.

62.   Similarly, the trial court in Borra v. Borra, 333 N.J. Super. 607, 614, 756 A.2d 647, 651 (Ch. Div. 2000) actually ruled that "when presented with a choice between parent's rights and children's rights, children's welfare and best interests will <u>always</u> be paramount". (Emphasis added).

63.   As a result of this holding that parents have NO fundamental rights in family court when there is a dispute between two parents, family judges such as Defendant Judge Paone routinely refuse to acknowledge any rights of parents in family court and strip parents of custody without a plenary hearing, or, as here, deny parents equal custody without hearings, or findings of fact.

64.   New Jersey's policy of interfering with parental rights based on nothing more than a vague "best interest" standard, without a showing of exceptional circumstances or unfitness, violates the fundamental constitutional rights of parents to the care, custody and control of children.

65.   This double standard articulated in *Sacharow*, of applying a far lower standard when stripping one parent of physical or legal custody in favor of another parent is contrary to well-established federal law. As the Third Circuit held *in B.S. v. Somerset*:

> From the parent's perspective, there may be little meaningful difference between instances in which the state removes a child and takes her into state custody and those in which the state shifts custody from one parent to another, as occurred here. In either case, the government has implicated a fundamental liberty interest of the parent who loses custody.

B.S., 704 F.3d at 272; *see also Stanley v. Illinois*, 405 U.S. 645, 649 (1972) ("Stanley was entitled to a hearing on his fitness as a parent before his children were taken from him[.]")

66.   As the Court went on to explain in *Stanley*:

> Under Illinois law, therefore, while the children of all parents can be taken from them in neglect proceedings, that is only after notice, hearing, and proof of such unfitness as a parent as amounts to neglect, an unwed father is uniquely subject to the more simplistic dependency proceeding. By use of this proceeding, the State, on showing that the father was not married to the mother, need not prove unfitness in fact, because it is presumed at law. Thus, the unwed father's claim of parental qualification is avoided as 'irrelevant.'

Id. at 650.

67.   When New Jersey seeks to strip both parents of custody they only do so after notice, discovery, hearing, appointed counsel for the indigent, and proof of unfitness, but in the context of an inter-parent dispute Defendants treat the parent's fundamental rights as nonexistent or irrelevant. This practice is unconstitutional.

68.   Frequently family court judges do not articulate what standard of proof was being applied, they appear to have applied a mere preponderance of the evidence standard at best. Frequently, custody is restricted based on nothing more than unspecified "concerns."

69.   In *Santosky v. Kramer*, 455 U.S. 745, 769, 102 S. Ct. 1388, 1403 (1982) the U.S. Supreme Court mandated a clear and convincing evidence standard when the state interferes with a parent's fundamental rights to the care, custody and control of children. *Troxell v. Granville*, 120 S. Ct. 2054 (2002) (holding that "best interest of the children" could not trump fundamental constitutional rights).

70.   Accordingly, Defendants' application of less than a clear and convincing standard to deprive one parent of custody is unconstitutional. It is widespread enough to constitute a policy as articulated in Sacharow v. Sacharow, 826 A.2d 710, 721 (N.J. 2003).

71.   Declaratory relief alone appears to be inadequate as Declaratory Judgment may not stop Defendant and successors from continuing to violate rights of Plaintiffs.

Relief

WHEREFORE, Plaintiffs request declaratory and injunctive relief against all Defendants that the "best interest" standard is unconstitutional when used to deprive parents of fundamental rights and that the policy of requiring a fit parent to prove change circumstances to achieve 50/50 custody is unconstitutional;

Costs and attorneys' fees as provided under federal law;

Such other relief as the Court determines to be just and appropriate.

Count III
DECLARATORY JUDGMENT

72.   Plaintiffs re-allege previous paragraphs as fully restated.

73.   Plaintiffs seek declaratory relief pursuant to the Declaratory Judgment Act, 28 U.S.C. § 2201

74.   Plaintiff remains in the New Jersey family court jurisdiction and will remain subject to custody orders of the family court until the minor A.P. turns 18-years old. As such they remain subject to the deprivation of their fundamental rights at any time given the prevalence of the above described treatment.

75.   Plaintiffs seek declaratory judgment that fundamental rights, including parental rights, First and Fourth Amendment rights may not be taken away without due process merely because they are in family court.

Relief

WHEREFORE, Plaintiffs request:

Declaratory relief;

Costs and attorneys' fees as provided under federal law;

Such other relief as the Court determines to be just and appropriate.

Respectfully Submitted,

Paul A. Clark, Esquire (PC4900)
10 Huron Ave, #1M
Jersey City, NJ 07306
(202) 368 5435

6. **Another Great Lawsuit Filed in United States District Court for the District of New Jersey**

PREPARED BY THE COURT

TUHIN PANDYA,	:	Superior Court of New Jersey
	:	Chancery Division, Family Part
Plaintiff,	:	Middlesex County
	:	
v.	:	Docket No.: FM-12-1499-12H
	:	
ROOPAL SHAH,	:	CIVIL ACTION
	:	
Defendant.	:	**ORDER**

THIS MATTER having been opened to the Court by Motion filed on April 29, 2014, by Plaintiff, Tuhin Pandya, represented by Paul A. Clark, Esq.; and an Opposition and Cross-Motion having been filed by Defendant, Roopal Shah, represented by Kenneth A. White, Esq.; and Defendant having filed a Reply Certification; and the Court having considered the papers submitted; and good cause having been shown:

IT IS on this 29th day of March 2015, in accordance with the attached Statement of Reasons, **ORDERED:**

1. Plaintiff's motion for shared custody of the parties' child, A____ (D.O.B. ___12), is **DENIED WITHOUT PREJUDICE** for lack of jurisdiction;

2. Plaintiff's motion to recalculate child support based on all of Defendant's available income, or, in the alternative, to reconsider the Court's April 17, 2015, Order regarding child support, is **DENIED WITHOUT PREJUDICE** for lack of jurisdiction;

3. Plaintiff's motion to schedule a plenary hearing and compel discovery for the purpose of determining Defendant's available income and assets is **DENIED WITHOUT PREJUDICE** for lack of jurisdiction;

4. Plaintiff's motion for counsel fees and costs is **DENIED WITHOUT PREJUDICE**;

Exhibit 1 to Pandya Complaint p. 1

5. Defendant's request that the Court find Plaintiff in violation of R. 1:4-8 and/or impose sanctions against Plaintiff for filing frivolous litigation is **DENIED WITHOUT PREJUDICE** for lack of jurisdiction;

6. Defendant's cross-motion to compel Plaintiff to disclose and provide proof of how he obtained private, privileged communication(s) between Defendant and her former attorney, Gerry Resnick, Esq., is **DENIED WITHOUT PREJUDICE** for lack of jurisdiction;

7. Defendant's cross-motion to quash any and all subpoenas previously served by Plaintiff is **DENIED WITHOUT PREJUDICE** for lack of jurisdiction;

8. Defendant's cross-motion to enforce and find Plaintiff in violation of litigant's rights under paragraph 16 of the JOD, which directs both parties to maintain, individually, "a minimum of Two Hundred and Fifty Thousand Dollar [*sic*] ($250,000) in life insurance benefits naming the minor child born of the marriage as beneficiary and the [other party] as trustee over said funds," is **GRANTED IN PART** as to enforcement, but **DENIED IN PART** as to a finding of a violation. Within fourteen (14) days of the return date of this Order, both parties shall take any and all steps necessary to establish a life insurance policy for A█████'s *sole* benefit, naming the other party as *sole* trustee. Upon either party's non-compliance, the other party may file a certification with the Court, requesting monetary sanctions and a bench warrant for the disobedient party's arrest;

9. Defendant's cross-motion for counsel fees and costs is **DENIED WITHOUT PREJUDICE**;

10. Any other claims for relief not expressly addressed in the Court's Order are **DENIED WITHOUT PREJUDICE**;

11. All other aspects of previous Orders not altered by this Order remain in effect;

Exhibit 1 to Pandya Complaint p. 2

12. A copy of this Order was sent to the parties' respective counsel by facsimile and regular mail on this date.

_____
HON. JOSEPH PAONE, J.S.C.

Exhibit 1 to Pandya Complaint p. 3

Statement of Reasons

I. Custody (paragraphs 1-3)

Plaintiff moves to modify custody. In support, Plaintiff claims that the PSA provided for custody and parenting time only through 2014. Plaintiff also provides the transcript from a December 11, 2012, hearing, during which The Hon. Andrea Carter-Latimer told the parties that they were "free to make the appropriate application [to modify custody] at the appropriate time" – *i.e.*, after the PSA's custody and parenting time provisions expired (Pl.'s Ex. 1). Plaintiff also moves to recalculate child support and, in the alternative, to reconsider this Court's April 17, 2015, Order regarding child support.

However, Plaintiff filed a Notice of Appeal to the Appellate Division to challenge this Court's April 17, 2015, Order regarding child support, depriving this Court of jurisdiction to award new relief. Under R. 2:9-1(a), which governs the control by the Appellate Division of proceedings pending appeal, provides as follows:

[T]he supervision and control of the proceedings on appeal or certification shall be in the appellate court from the time the appeal is taken or the notice of petition for certification filed. The trial court, however, shall have continuing jurisdiction to enforce judgments and orders pursuant to R. 1:10 and as otherwise provided.

See also Rolnick v. Rolnick, 262 N.J. Super. 343, 365 (App. Div. 1993) ("Except as to the extent of enforcement and except as otherwise expressly provided for by the rule, the ordinary effect of the filing of the notice of appeal is to deprive the [trial] court below of jurisdiction to act further in the matter unless directed to do so by the appellate court."). In the instant action, Plaintiff moves to modify custody and child support, and to reconsider the same decision he has appealed to the Appellate Division. Thus, this Court is deprived of jurisdiction to hear the merits of

Exhibit 1 to Pandya Complaint p. 4

Plaintiff's motion. Likewise, this Court does not have jurisdiction to decide the merits of Defendant's cross-motion, except as to her enforcement application regarding life insurance.

II.   Life Insurance (paragraph 8)

Defendant cross-moves to enforce litigant's rights under paragraph 16 of the PSA, which requires both parties to maintain, individually, "a minimum of Two Hundred and Fifty Thousand Dollar [sic] ($250,000) in life insurance benefits naming the minor child born of the marriage as beneficiary and the [other party] as trustee over said funds." (Def.'s Ex. G). According to Defendant, she has repeatedly asked Plaintiff for proof that he secured such life insurance benefits to no avail.

In opposition, Plaintiff provides copies of several letters to Defendant, with proof of having delivered the letters to Defendant (Pl.'s Reply Ex. 2). In the letters, Plaintiff asks Defendant when she would be available to review and sign a life insurance trust for A████'s benefit. Plaintiff also claims that Defendant has refused to provide her life insurance policy for Plaintiff's signature.

In paragraph 8 of the October 28, 2014, Order, this Court ordered both parties to provide proof to the other that he or she has obtained a life insurance policy for A████'s sole benefit and named the other as trustee thereof. Based on Plaintiff's proven correspondence to Defendant regarding arrangements to review and/or sign a life insurance trust for A████'s benefit, the Court cannot find that Plaintiff has violated Defendant's rights. However, it appears that neither party has complied with the mandate to provide proof of having obtained the policies. Tellingly, Defendant does not list a life insurance policy in Part E of her updated CIS (Def.'s Ex. I), and she fails to provide any proof that she even attempted to obtain the requisite life insurance.

Exhibit 1 to Pandya Complaint p. 5

Accordingly, the Court finds it appropriate to direct both parties to take any and all necessary steps to establish the requisite life insurance policies no later than fourteen (14) days after the return date of this Order, subject to monetary sanctions and/or an arrest warrant for non-compliance.

III.   Counsel Fees and Costs (paragraphs 4, 9)

Both parties move for counsel fees and costs. When deciding whether to award counsel fees in a post-judgment action, the Court considers, among other things, the requesting party's need, the requested party's financial ability to pay and the requesting party's good faith in instituting or defending the action. R. 5:3-5(c); Williams v. Williams, 59 N.J. 229, 233 (1971). Fee awards for pure enforcement motions governed by R. 1:10 are not subject to the factors established in R. 5:3-5(c), but are still subject to a reasonableness standard.

While the parties' respective financial positions remain disputed (on appeal), they have both acted in bad faith in filing and defending their applications. Plaintiff filed a motion with this Court, in part, to reconsider its prior Order after appealing that same Order to the Appellate Division, forcing Defendant to incur unnecessary legal fees in responding thereto. Defendant, in turn, cross-moved to enforce the life insurance provision of the PSA that he has yet to prove his own compliance with. Accordingly, the Court does not find it reasonable to award either party attorney's fees incurred in filing and/or defending the instant matter.

Exhibit 1 to Pandya Complaint p. 6

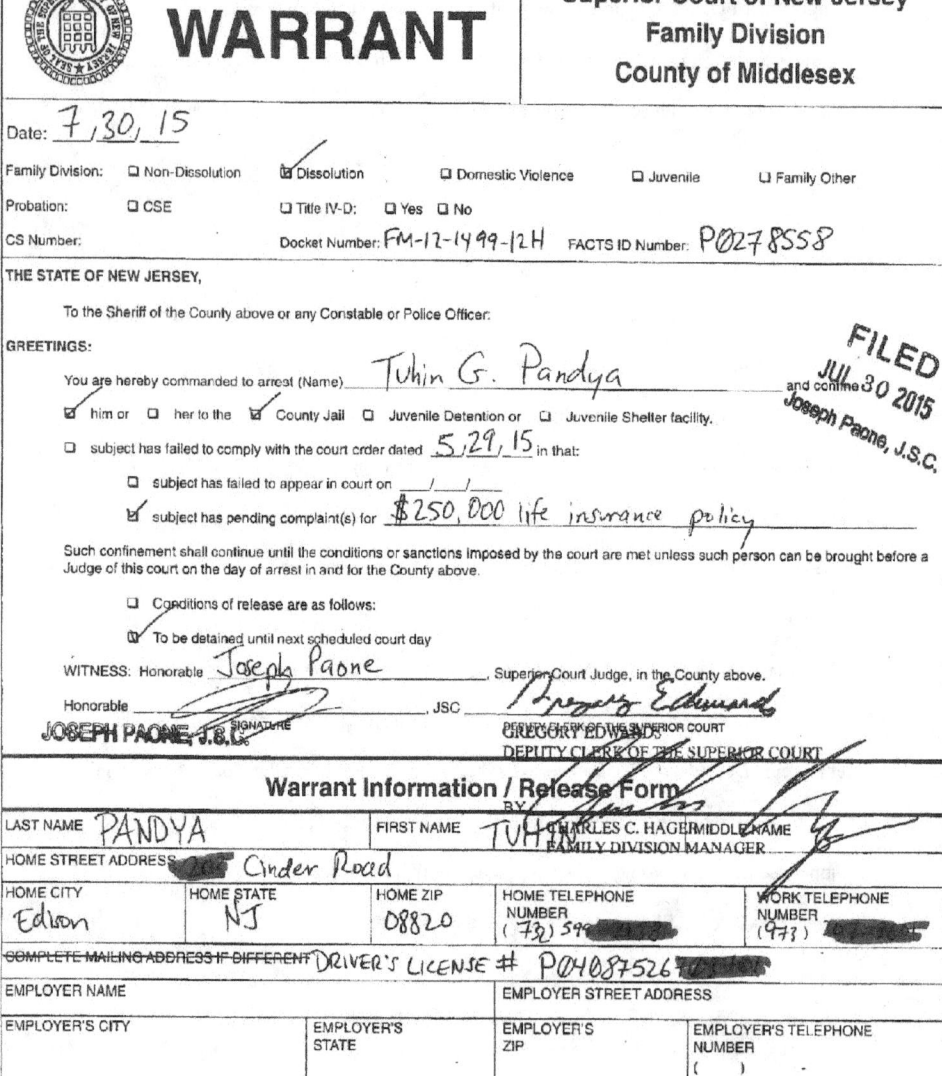

WARRANT

Superior Court of New Jersey
Family Division
County of Middlesex

Date: 7, 30, 15

Family Division:	☐ Non-Dissolution	☒ Dissolution	☐ Domestic Violence	☐ Juvenile	☐ Family Other

Probation: ☐ CSE   ☐ Title IV-D: ☐ Yes ☐ No

CS Number: Docket Number: FM-12-1499-12H   FACTS ID Number: P0278558

THE STATE OF NEW JERSEY,

To the Sheriff of the County above or any Constable or Police Officer:

GREETINGS:

You are hereby commanded to arrest (Name) _Tuhin G. Pandya_

☒ him or ☐ her to the ☒ County Jail ☐ Juvenile Detention or ☐ Juvenile Shelter facility.

☐ subject has failed to comply with the court order dated _5, 29, 15_ in that:

　☐ subject has failed to appear in court on __/__/__

　☒ subject has pending complaint(s) for _$250,000 life insurance policy_

Such confinement shall continue until the conditions or sanctions imposed by the court are met unless such person can be brought before a Judge of this court on the day of arrest in and for the County above.

　☐ Conditions of release are as follows:

　☒ To be detained until next scheduled court day

WITNESS: Honorable _Joseph Paone_, Superior Court Judge, in the County above.

Honorable _____, JSC _____

JOSEPH PAONE, J.S.C.   SIGNATURE

GREGORY EDWARDS
DEPUTY CLERK OF THE SUPERIOR COURT

FILED
JUL 30 2015
Joseph Paone, J.S.C.

Warrant Information / Release Form

BY _____
CHARLES C. HAGER
FAMILY DIVISION MANAGER

LAST NAME _PANDYA_   FIRST NAME _TUH_   MIDDLE NAME

HOME STREET ADDRESS _Cinder Road_

HOME CITY	HOME STATE	HOME ZIP	HOME TELEPHONE NUMBER	WORK TELEPHONE NUMBER
Edison	NJ	08820	(78) 59_____	(973) _____

COMPLETE MAILING ADDRESS IF DIFFERENT   DRIVER'S LICENSE # _P04087526_____

EMPLOYER NAME	EMPLOYER STREET ADDRESS

EMPLOYER'S CITY	EMPLOYER'S STATE	EMPLOYER'S ZIP	EMPLOYER'S TELEPHONE NUMBER ( ) -

SUBJECT DESCRIPTION	DATE OF BIRTH	SEX	RACE	HEIGHT	WEIGHT	HAIR	EYES	SS#
		M	Asian/Oriental	5'07"	150	Black	Black	

PURGE AMOUNT PAID: $ IF APPLICABLE AND DEFENDANT IS RELEASED	SIGNATURE (Sheriff Designee)	Return this warrant to:	☐ IV-D Probation _____ ☐ Family Division _____

FORM DESIGNED BY: FORM UNIT (609) 984-3147 / TRIAL COURT SUPPORT OPERATIONS / ADMINISTRATIVE OFFICE OF THE COURTS

Exhibit 2 to Pandya Complaint

IN THE UNITED STATES DISTRICT COURT
FOR THE DISTRICT OF NEW JERSEY

SCOTT EDELGLASS, SAMIR JOSHI, for)
himself and as parent of J.J., J.J. and)
J.J.,YEHUDA BEN LITTON,)
SURENDER MALHAN, for himself)
and as parent of E.M and V.M.,)
ANTONIO QUINLAN for himself and as)
parent of K.Q., for themselves and on)
behalf of all others similarly situated,)
)
        Plaintiffs,)
)
        v.)
)
STATE OF NEW JERSEY, MICHELLE M.)
SMITH (in her official capacity as Clerk,)
Superior Court of New Jersey))
BURLINGTON COUNTY, JOHN L CULL, JR)
(in his official capacity as Presiding Judge)
Chancery Div., Family Part, Burlington)
County), HUDSON COUNTY, MAUREEN)
SUGLUIZO (in her official capacity as)
Presiding Judge, Chancery Div., Family)
Part, Hudson County) OCEAN COUNTY,)
PATRICIA B. ROE (in her official)
capacity as Presiding Judge, Chancery)
Div., Family Part, Ocean County),)
)
        _____Defendants._____)

No._____

Jury Trial Demanded

COMPLAINT

Jurisdiction

1.   This Court has jurisdiction over this matter under 28 U.S.C. §1331. Plaintiffs maintain this action under 42 U.S.C. §1983, on their own behalf and on behalf of all others similarly situated. The State, Counties and individual defendants, in their official capacity deprived Plaintiffs of liberty under color of law by depriving parents of the fundamental right to the care, custody and control of their minor children without affording them even minimal procedural protections guaranteed by the United States Constitution.

Summary

2.   Plaintiffs seek declaratory and injunctive relief under Federal Rule of Civil Procedure 23(a) and (b)(2) on behalf of all persons who have been or in the future will be deprived of child custody by Defendants without a prompt and full hearing; as well as monetary damages against County Defendants which under color of law deprived Plaintiffs of custody without a prompt and full hearing, and in violation of the Fourteenth Amendment.

Parties

3.   Scott Edelglass is an adult residing in Ocean County. He is father of Z.E., now 19-years-old, but who was a minor during the events described herein.

4.   Yehuda Ben Litton is an adult residing in Ocean County. He is father of L.L, now 15-years-old.

5.   Samir Joshi is an adult residing in Pennsylvania. He is father of the minor children J.J. (age 14), J.J. (age 12). and J.J. (age 10). Joshi brings this suit on behalf of himself and his minor children.

6.   Surrender Malhan is an adult residing in Hudson County, Jersey City, New Jersey. He is father of the minor children E.M. and V.M., ages 7 and 4. Malhan brings this suit on behalf of himself and his minor children.

7.   Antonio Quinlan is an adult residing in Hudson County, Jersey City, New Jersey. He is father of the minor child K.Q. Quinlan is able to bring this suit on behalf of K.Q. because the Order denying him legal custody of K.Q. is null and void.

8.   Defendants, Burlington County, Hudson County, and Ocean County ("County Defendants") are subdivisions of the State of New Jersey and are a "person" in all respects within the meaning of 42 U.S.C. §1983. County defendants participate fully in enforcing superior court orders through a variety of county agencies including law enforcement agencies, child welfare agencies and county visitation offices.

9.   Individual Defendants sued in their official capacity are officials tasked with administration and enforcing New Jersey law, and are sued in their

capacity as administrators tasked with enforcing policies which deny plaintiffs constitutional rights under color of law; they are persons within the meaning of 42 U.S.C. §1983 with respect to declarative and injunctive relief sought in this case.

Statement of Facts

10.   Defendants have established policies, procedures, and precedents denying parents a full and prompt hearing when stripping one parent of physical and legal custody and giving full physical and legal custody to another parent. This is a clear violation of the Fourteenth Amendment to the United States' Constitution under color of law.

Facts Relevant to Plaintiff Edelglass

11.   Plaintiff Scott Edelglass's son, Z.E. was born in the Spring of 1994. The mother of the child was Erin Fisher. Within a few months of the birth of Z.E., Edelglass discovered there were serious threats to Z.E.'s safety in the home of Erin and he petitioned Monmouth County for custody. This was the start of a prolonged custody dispute that would last for the next eighteen years.

12.   In December of 1997, Erin filed a motion in Monmouth County Family Court seeking sole custody of Z.E. As a result of this motion Erin was granted "sole custody" of Z.E. Moreover, Edelglass was only permitted to have supervised visitation with Z.E. for the next two years.

13.   Although there were numerous and extremely serious allegations regarding the safety of Z.E. in Erin's custody, Erin was granted full custody and Edelglass's custody severely restricted without a plenary hearing. Edelglass was not permitted a full opportunity to present evidence or challenge the evidence against him.

14.   In April 1998, Edelglass petitioned the court to permit him unsupervised visitation, but this request was denied. Again the Court failed to afford Edelglass a plenary hearing. The court did not explain the basis for continuing to deny Edelgrass unsupervised visitation, but presumably credited the unsubstantiated allegations made against him.

15.   For the next ten years, until Z.E. was old enough to decide to see his father on his own, Edelglass's parenting time with his child was severely restricted due to the actions and willful inactions of the Monmouth County Family courts and Monmouth counties agencies. For example, in the Fall and Winter of 2005 to 2006, Edelglass was permitted only a few hours every few weeks with Z.E., with the exception of a few additional hours the night before Thanksgiving. In March 2006, Edelglass asked the Court to schedule a hearing to resolve this problem, but Edelglass's parenting time remained severely restricted based on unsubstantiated allegations and the stipulation that he not use his last name, talk about his religion, or ask his son about his grades if he were to continue to see his son even on a limited basis.

16.   These severe restrictions on Edelglass's ability to interact with his son likely have caused significant and long-lasting damage to father-child relationship.

Facts Relevant to Plaintiff Joshi

17.   Joshi was married to Christine Joshi in Pennsylvania. The children of the marriage were born in Pennsylvania and Christine filed for divorce in Pennsylvania. In or around 2012 Christine asked New Jersey to take jurisdiction.

18.   On or about June 22, 2012 Christine filed an Order to Show Cause in New Jersey Superior Court, Burlington County. Joshi was not properly served and did not appear for this proceeding. At the proceeding, Christine gave testimony, but her testimony was based largely on hearsay evidence, alleging what a police officer supposedly told Christine. The Court set a return date on the Order to Show Cause for July 12, 2012.

19.   Joshi did not have notice of the July 12 proceeding until a few days before the hearing. Joshi contacted the Court and requested a continuance due to the fact that Joshi's father had just passed away a few days earlier and Joshi was in the midst of funeral arrangements for his father.

20.   Joshi appeared telephonically in Court July 12, 2012 and reiterated his need for a continuance as he was in the middle of funeral arrangements and

religious services for his father. Joshi also objected to New Jersey asserting jurisdiction pointing out that the Order from Pennsylvania transferring jurisdiction was on appeal.

21.   At this July 12 proceeding, Joshi was not allowed to cross examine Christine. Due to the short notice and death in the family, Joshi did not have time to prepare evidence to submit, nor obtain counsel.

22.   The Court told Joshi to hand over physical custody of the children later that day. By written Order dated July 12, 2012, the Court "suspended parenting time until [Joshi] provides assurance that he will return the parties' children, and the Court issues another order."

23.   Joshi requested that this Order be revised to give him full and equal custody. In response in an Order dated December 4, 2012 the Court slightly modified the earlier Order but only permitted "supervised visitation through the Burlington County Supervised Visitation Program." December 4, 2012, Order. No plenary hearing was held prior to entry of this Order.

24.   During the summer of 2013, Joshi again demanded full and equal custody of this custody, and requested a full plenary hearing. In an Order dated July 26, 2013 Joshi's request for a plenary hearing was denied. The Court Order granted limited parenting time to Joshi of 14 hours a week--four hours on Wednesday evenings and ten hours on Saturday.

25.   As of the filing of this Compliant, Joshi has been permitted little or no visitation with his children for more than a year without a plenary hearing. Joshi currently has joint legal custody of the children.

26.   The severe restrictions on Joshi's ability to parent likely have caused significant and long-lasting damage to father-child relationships.

Facts Relevant to Plaintiff Litton

27.   Litton was married to Linda Litton in 1982. They had one child, a son, L.L., born in 1998. The parties separated in 2004 but Litton and his wife agreed to a 50/50 custody arrangement.

28.   On January 10, 2008 a Judgment of Divorce was granted in Monmouth County Superior Court, Family Division. Custody was divided 50/50 between

them, however, Linda denied Litton any time with his son. Immediately following the judgment, jurisdiction in the case was transferred to Ocean County. On May 7, 2008, Litton asked the Ocean County Court to enforce the 50/50 custody arrangement to which the parties had previously agreed.

29.   Litton's son was 10-years-old at this time and the court conducted an in camera interview of the child without the parties present. After the in camera interview the Court ruled that Litton's parenting time should be suspended indefinitely.

30.   In an Order dated May 8, 2008 the Court directed that Litton's visitation "is suspended pending further order of court."

31.   Litton's right to be with his son was suspended indefinitely without a plenary hearing. Litton had no opportunity to challenge whatever allegation had been made against him, or to call witnesses or refute whatever allegations had been made that concerned the judge.

32.   This Order remained in effect until March 2010 when the Court conducted a full hearing and issued a new Order which allowed Litton to see his son a few hours each week.

33.   The Order issued by the court on March 24, 2010 concluded that "Linda has substantially poisoned L[]'s perception of [Litton], thereby causing L[] to reject his father. . . . I find that she has manipulated L[] to make the implementation of parenting time with [Litton] almost impossible."

34.   The March 24, 2010 Order was "too little, too late." Had the Court convened a plenary hearing back in 2008 these facts would have been uncovered then.

35.   For nearly two years, from May 2008 until March 2010 Litton only saw his son once. As it was, the State stripped Litton of contact with his son based on unsubstantiated allegations that Litton was not permitted to refute. These severe restrictions on Litton's ability to see his son likely have caused significant and long-lasting damage to father-child relationship.

Facts Relevant to Plaintiff Malhan

36.   On February 24, 2011, Alina Myronova, mother of Malhan's minor children filed an Order to Show Cause in Hudson County Family Court asking that full physical and legal custody of the children be given to her. Myronova claimed that Malhan was an unfit parent who could not take care of children. Myronova made these allegations in an affidavit.

37.   Malhan had less than two hours' notice of a legal proceeding and had no time to seek legal advice or obtain counsel.

38.   Malhan when appearing before the family part judge contested all of Myronova's allegations about his alleged unfitness as a parent. Malhan stated that Myronova was lying. Malhan was not permitted to cross examine Myronova.

39.   Malhan told the court that he wished to present evidence to refute the allegations made by Myronova, specifically he stated that he had audio recordings, photographs and videos which could document his ability to parent and would show that Myronova was lying. The court did not permit Malhan to present any evidence.

40.   Malhan told the Court that Myronova had in her possession documents, including bank records, which would prove that she was lying about some of her allegations and asked the Court to require Myronova to produce these records; the court refused to order the production of said documents.

41.   On February 24, 2011, the Court stripped Malhan of physical and legal custody ordering Myronova to assume full legal and physical custody of the two children.

42.   Malhan was permitted only one hour a week of supervised visitation.

43.   Although the Court in Malhan's case did not explain the basis for the decision, counties throughout New Jersey apply a preponderance of the evidence standard, and thus strip parents of custody based on no more than a showing of "best interests of the child" by a mere preponderance of evidence when custody is transferred to another parent.

44.   The Hudson County court set a further return date of April 1, 2011.
On April 1, the court still did not permit Malhan to cross examine Myronova
and there was no plenary hearing. The Court continued to deny Malhan
legal and physical custody of the two children keeping Myronova as sole
legal and physical custodian. Malhan was permitted several hours a week of
unsupervised visitation with his children.

45.   Myronova kept sole legal and physical custody of the two children for
sixteen months, until June 2012 when she agreed to permit joint custody.
During this sixteen month period Malhan was never granted a plenary
hearing.

46.   Malhan ultimately prevailed in obtaining joint physical and legal
custody, with the Court ruling that Myronova's previous objections to Malhan
taking care of the children had been without basis.

Facts Relevant to Plaintiff Quinlan

47.   In December, 2010 Quinlan was stripped of legal custody of his minor
child, K.Q., who was 13-years-old at the time. This was a result of a motion
filed by Quinlan's ex-wife Kayoi Quinlan Hasabe.

48.   In an order dated December 16, 2010, the Hudson County Superior
Court, Family Division, stripped Quinlan of legal custody without a full
hearing and in violation of due process. Although there was a court
proceeding on December 3, 2010 before the Court terminated Quinlan's
legal custody of his child, Quinlan was not permitted to testify or present
evidence in his own defense at this hearing. For example, the Court relied
on hearsay emails written by Quinlan's father, Robert Quinlan, who never
testified. The Court relied on these emails as evidence that Quinlan
harassed Hasabe. Not only were these out-of court statements by Robert
Quinlan used as a basis for terminating Quinlan's legal custody, Quinlan was
not permitted to rebut or explain his father's emails.

49.   Although there were numerous disputes of fact contested by Quinlan,
when Quinlan attempted to explain why various accusation were not true the

Court admonished Quinlan: "I've read everything that you've given me, there can't possibly be another thing that you need to tell me."

50.   Although Quinlan's ex-wife, Hasebe, appeared at the hearing she did not testify, and Quinlan was not able to cross examine her. The Court apparently relied on Hasebe's certifications. The Court also relied on numerous contradictory letters and other unsworn statements made by Hasebe.

51.   The court terminated Quinlan's parental custody without a full hearing at which he was permitted to testify, present evidence and confront witnesses against him.

52.   New Jersey denied Quinlan due process rights in other significant ways. Apparently through an "administrative error" New Jersey entered an Order in a national database that indicates that Quinlan is subject to a restraining Order preventing him from having any contact with his daughter. This incorrect entry in the federal database has repeatedly caused Quinlan to be detained, and significantly interferes with Quinlan's ability to be with his daughter. For example, if he reenters the country with his daughter he risks being detained or even arrested.

53.   Quinlan has repeatedly demanded that New Jersey and/or its subdivisions correct this error, which has been ongoing for years. However, New Jersey and/or its subdivisions has refused to take any action. This repeated refusal to correct this interference with Quinlan's ability to parent his child indicates an ongoing policy failing to protect the parental rights of people like Quinlan.

54.   In addition to other relief sought, Quinlan requests injunctive relief directing New Jersey to correct this apparent administrative error.

55.   Furthermore, during litigation, Quinlan's wife retained a law firm that Quinlan had previously consulted with about his divorce case. Quinlan had not only consulted with this firm but had paid them a $2,000 retainer for their advice. Quinlan brought this to the attention of the court even providing a carbon copy of the check written to the law firm. However, the court refused to even make a ruling on this issue, apparently because the

attorney with the conflict of interest was becoming a judge. The attorney with this conflict of interest, i fact, became a family court judge in the same county and division as the presiding judge who had refused to address Quinlan's complaint about a conflict of interest. Thus the Court denied Quinlan due process by refusing to grant a motion that would have been detrimental to a fellow judge.

56.   Further, the Court denied and continues to deny Quinlan due process and his Second Amendment rights by ordering him not to possess any weapons. The Court issued this Order without any type of hearing on the issue or any showing that Quinlan's possession of weapons presented a danger. Thus Quinlan demands a declaratory and injunctive relief that the State and county may not deprive a person the fundamental right to keep and bear arms without showing the Order is necessary on a case by case basis, and the Order is at the very least narrowly tailored to an important state interest.

Facts Relevant to all Plaintiffs

57.   Upon information and belief, the denial of prompt and full custody hearing in the context of transferring custody from one parent to another is widespread throughout the state and country. *See, e.g*, "Parental Rights and Due Process" in 1 THE JOURNAL OF LAW AND FAMILY STUDIES, 2:123-150 (1999) (noting the widespread violation of due process in the family law context); *B.S. v. Somerset County*, 704 F.3d 250, 275 (3d Cir. 2013) ("[T]he County essentially admits . . . the County has a custom of removing children from a parent's home without conducting a prompt post-removal hearing if another parent can take custody" and holding that this violated the Fourteenth Amendment); S.M. v. K.M., ---- A. 2d. -----, A-6096-12T3, 2013 WL 6799313 (N.J. Super. Ct. App. Div. 2013) (describing a case where parental rights of father were terminated without a plenary hearing or even an explanation); *Sacharow v. Sacharow*, 177 N.J. 62, 79, 826 A.2d 710, 721 (2003) (holding that a parent has no fundamental right to the custody of

children in the family law context because "[i]t is not a third party or the State that seeks to intrude into the protected sphere of family autonomy.").

Count I
Deprivation of Fundamental Rights under Color of Law

58.   Plaintiffs re-allege previous paragraphs as fully restated.

59.   It is clearly established federal law that a parent may not be deprived of his or her fundamental rights to the care, custody and control of minor children without due process. Minors have a reciprocal right not to be separated from their parents absent a compelling reason. New Jersey and the County Defendants violated the substantive and procedural rights of Plaintiffs by interfering with the care custody and control of minor children without affording Plaintiffs the most basic due process rights, including adequate notice, the right to counsel, the right to cross examine accusers, and the right to present evidence in one's defense.

60.   Defendants further stripped Plaintiffs of the their fundamental rights based on a mere "preponderance of the evidence" standard, and furthermore, the State and its Courts fail to even allow proper discovery or court room procedures to uncover evidence. Thus not only is the state using an impermissible "preponderance of the evidence" rather than "clear and convincing evidence" but it not even permitting a fair playing field for what evidence is presented.

61.   Defendants have established policies, procedures, and precedents denying parents a full and prompt hearing when stripping one parent of physical and legal custody and giving full physical and legal custody to another parent. This is a clear violation of the Fourteenth Amendment to the United States' Constitution under color of law.

62.   The Hudson County Family Court ultimately determined that Malhan was a fit parent and that the allegation made against him were false; however, had the State and County permitted a full and prompt hearing Plaintiff Malhan would have demonstrated that the allegations against him were unfounded and his children would have been returned to his custody

within a matter of days rather than the sixteen months the process
ultimately took.

63.   The State and Hudson County also denied Quinlan the fundamental
right to the care custody and control of his children, by denying him full and
equal custody with his ex-wife for over a year without due process. His child
has also been substantially denied access to her father for over a year,
without due process.

64.   69. The State and Burlington County have denied Joshi the
fundamental right to the care custody and control of his children, by denying
him full and equal custody of his children for over a year without due
process. Most importantly, his young impressionable children have also
been substantially denied access to and alienated from their father for over
sixteen months, without due process

65.   The State and Middlesex County have significantly interfered with
Smith's the fundamental rights to the care custody and control of his child,
by denying him equal custody for a year without due process. E.S. has also
been substantially denied full access to his father for over a year, without
due process.

66.   As a result of the above deprivation of rights, the Plaintiffs have
suffered profound injuries; the bonds between parent and child have been
perhaps permanently injured in ways that are not quantifiable. Plaintiffs
have suffered emotional pain and mental anguish as a result of said
deprivations over a period of sixteen months.

                                    Relief
WHEREFORE, Plaintiffs request damages against County Defendants in an
amount to be determined at trial;

        Declaratory and injunctive relief against all Defendants on behalf of all
persons who have been or in the future will be deprived of the physical or
legal custody of their children without a prompt and full hearing;
(declaratory relief should Order New Jersey to provide a plenary hearing

within ten days to any parent who has their right to the care custody and control of their children reduced through State action);

Costs and attorneys' fees as provided under federal law;

Such other relief as the Court determines to be just and appropriate.

Respectfully Submitted,

Paul A. Clark, Esquire NJ # 04261-2011
10 Huron Ave, #1M
Jersey City, NJ 07306
(202) 368 5435

www.ingramcontent.com/pod-product-compliance
Lightning Source LLC
Chambersburg PA
CBHW081618220526
45468CB00010B/2934